I'm nobody: Who are you?

Poems by Emily Dickinson

I'm nobody! Who are you?

Poems by Emily Dickinson

Edited by
Edric S. Mesmer

With an introduction
by Virginia Euwer Wolff

SCHOLASTIC INC.
New York Toronto London Auckland Sydney
Mexico City New Delhi Hong Kong Buenos Aires

No part of this work may be reproduced in whole or in part, or stored in a retrieval system, or transmitted in any form or by any means, electronic, mechanical, photocopying, recording, or otherwise, without written permission of the publisher. For information regarding permission, write to Scholastic Inc., Attention: Permissions Department, 555 Broadway, New York, NY 10012.

ISBN 0-439-29576-9

12 11 10 9 8 7 6 5 4 3 2 1   2 3 4 5 6 7/0

Printed in the U.S.A.   01

INTRODUCTION

On my studio wall I have a quotation from Emily Dickinson: "My business is circumference." I walk past it, wondering just how she meant that. I know that if I put my arms up in a sort of circle I'm making something of a circumference. Is that what she meant? To surround? To surround what? The world? All the laundry and pencil-sharpening and drudgery and excitement, all the discoveries and war and peace, all the birth and death and laughter and tears?

Did she mean she was trying to surround life in order to understand it?

Or in order to love it?

My guess is that she wanted to explore, to feel her way around everything, just by thinking about it all. For instance, to surround such a quick thing as a bird:

> A bird came down the walk:
> He did not know I saw:
> He bit an angle-worm in halves
> And ate the fellow, raw.

That word — "raw" — is a little bit startling. She forces us to concentrate on that cold, squishy meat. And later in the poem:

And he unrolled his feathers
And rowed him softer home

Once again, she has chosen such an unlikely word, "rowed." But ever since I found that poem, as I watch the robins outside my window, eating their worms raw and then "rowing" home through the waves of air, I'm able to see them so much more clearly.

And that's a poet's job: to hold up a different lens for us, enabling us to see the world in clearer focus than we could by ourselves.

The American poet Louise Glück has said that Emily Dickinson "allows us to overhear" her poetry.

Have a look at the first poem in this book. It seems almost to be whispered: a secret between confiding voices. "Are you nobody, too?" "Don't tell!" It almost feels as if we are untying one of the many bundles of unpublished poems that Miss Dickinson left behind when she died.

In this "I'm nobody!" poem, we can see both her solitude and her sense of fun. How "admiring" a bog can be when a frog announces it name over and over again. In fact, she managed to find personality in bees, snakes, insects, and fields of grasses. Did she just keep looking harder than most of us do, making them part of her "circumference"?

She tries to surround language. For instance, in putting words together oddly:

I never hear the word "escape"
Without a quicker blood,
A sudden expectation,
A flying attitude.

Haven't we all felt "a flying attitude" when we think of escaping something? And yet most of us wouldn't think of putting "flying" with "attitude." Miss Dickinson, such a bold experimenter, did. She snips words out of lines that we might leave in; she draws surprising comparisons all over the place ("hope is the thing with feathers"); she keeps drawing us close to whisper in our ear and then puts words in front of us that bewilder us completely, keeping her secrets to herself after all. And to the literary men of her time, her unusual word combinations and urgent punctuation pushing the poems forward were just too confusing. It may have been easier for them to ignore her poetry than to try to understand it. Thus, only a handful of her poems were published when she was alive, and 1,200 were found in meticulously sewn packets of pages at the time of her death.

One of the chief reasons for poets to exist — in my personal opinion — is to give us something to do when we feel so terrible about life that we just can't go on. Then it's time for sad songs, sad pictures, sad phrases. Miss Dickinson does very well here. How often have I lamented my own personal tragedies while I was reading her "certain slant of light"?

> There's a certain slant of light,
> On winter afternoons,
> That oppresses, like the weight
> Of cathedral tunes.

Oh, what comfort to know *somebody* feels as hopeless as I do!

> Heavenly hurt it gives us;
> We can find no scar,
> But internal difference
> Where the meanings are.

Oh, thank you, Emily, for understanding misery! That's it, exactly! Down in my insides, where my private meanings are, that *nobody* else feels!

The poem continues just as disconsolately as it began, only more so, and it's perfect for sobbing alone.

Socrates said, "The unexamined life is not worth living." And yet, sometimes well-meaning people tell us not to think about our terrible problems so much, that doing so will just make us feel worse. Well, I say play some sad music, gather together some comfort food, a blanket, a box of tissues, and this despairing poem; examine your life down to its most embarrassing details of rejection, isolation, and overwhelming melancholy. Call it poetry therapy.

Hint: This book contains other desolate poems, some that can leave me feeling forlorn for hours. You'll find them without my help.

Miss Dickinson's eager mind had room for giddy humor, too. Here's a note she sent her young nephew, Ned, after the town of Amherst and the Dickinson home had been broken into by thieves: "Burglaries have become so frequent, is it safe to leave the Golden Rule out at night?"

We've all seen the masks of comedy and tragedy; we know how just a slight movement of the mouth and eyes can make one into the other. Part of a poet's job is to show us this paradox in new ways. And this poet was especially good at it. She imagined her own death — or anybody's — and wrote:

I heard a fly buzz when I died;

She brought together two things: the ordinary housefly and the biggest mystery of all, death. She put them in one sentence. And, once we know the poem, it's a combination that's hard *not* to think about. All over the world, people are walking around with those words echoing in their minds every time a fly buzzes too close for comfort. Is it a joke? Or not? I imagine my own death as a tragic, consuming event. Don't you? But there's that fly, with its "uncertain, stumbling buzz," who doesn't care at all. In fact, it's waiting hungrily for my dead flesh.

And are we that way about death, too — "uncertain, stumbling"? Of course we are. Death is the one unsolvable mystery.

We often stumble, too, when we try to understand poetry. Some poems let us get them right away, and some hide their meanings just out of sight, teasing or challenging us to try to find them. Is the fly in this poem really a fly? Is it supposed to *mean* something far more huge? Does the fly *stand for* all the pettiness that surrounds us in our lives, which will disappear when we die? Does it stand for all the buzzing that our loved ones are doing about our death? We know that a housefly has an extremely short life; sometimes we joke about it, and at other times we feel quiet pity for it. In this poem, does Emily Dickinson bring the fly into the room where our deathbed stands in order to remind us of how short our lives are?

She never explained.

With Emily Dickinson's poetry, we're all slow to say, "Oh! I get it!" And then I always wonder: Do I really get it, or do I just *think* I get it?

Like all of us, she was trying very hard to understand what it means to be alive. Here's another quotation from her lively mind. "I am out with lanterns, looking for myself." Aren't we all?

Near my desk I keep a photo of Emily Dickinson's bedroom and writing table. The photograph reminds me that writing —yours, mine, ours—is important in our relationship with the world, even if no one else ever sees it. Even if it were to stay in bundles in our bedrooms, it would still have pungence, spunk, and heart — if only because we had the courage to put it on paper.

In our time, this secret woman who thought of life as "mystic territory" is listed in the Academy of American Poets, and crowds of eager tourists visit the large brick house she lived in at 280 Main Street in Amherst, Massachusetts.

Some thoughts on what to call her. I feel that calling her "Miss Dickinson" shows respect for her dignity and her veil of seclusion. But in the privacy of my own home, looking at the picture of her writing table on my windowsill and reading her "circumference" statement on my wall, I call her Emily. You'll decide what seems right for you. I think she would want it that way.

Go into these poems for the adventure of them. Burrow in and find a word or a phrase that intrigues you. Try beginning to piece it together with its neighboring words. Be Miss Dickinson's companion. Emily's companion. You'll find yourself making meanings that surprise you.

— Virginia Euwer Wolff

CONTENTS

I'm nobody! Who are you?
Are you nobody, too?
Then there's a pair of us — don't tell!
They'd banish us, you know.

How dreary to be somebody!
How public, like a frog
To tell your name the livelong day
To an admiring bog!

The way I read a letter's this:
'Tis first I lock the door,
And push it with my fingers next,
For transport to be sure.

And then I go the furthest off
To counteract a knock;
Then draw my little letter forth
And softly pick its lock

Then, glancing narrow at the wall,
And narrow at the floor,
For firm conviction of a mouse
Not exorcised before,

Peruse how infinite I am
To — no one that you know!
And sigh for lack of heaven, — but not
The heaven the creeds bestow.

To make a prairie it takes a clover
and one bee, —
One clover, and a bee,
And revery.
The revery alone will do
If bees are few.

Water is taught by thirst;
Land, by the oceans passed;
   Transport, by throe;
Peace, by its battles told;
Love, by memorial mould;
   Birds, by the snow.

The soul selects her own society,
Then shuts the door;
On her divine majority
Obtrude no more.

Unmoved, she notes the chariot's pausing
At her low gate;
Unmoved, an emperor is kneeling
Upon her mat.

I've known her from an ample nation
Choose one;
Then close the valves of her attention
Like stone.

A something in a summer's day,
As slow her flambeaux burn away,
Which solemnizes me.

A something in a summer's noon, —
An azure depth, a wordless tune,
Transcending ecstasy.

And still within a summer's night
A something so transporting bright,
I clap my hands to see;

Then veil my too inspecting face,
Lest such a subtle, shimmering grace
Flutter too far for me.

The wizard-fingers never rest,
The purple brook within the breast
Still chafes its narrow bed;

Still rears the East her amber flag,
Guides still the sun along the crag
His caravan of red,

Like flowers that heard the tale of dews,
But never deemed the dripping prize
Awaited their low brows;

Or bees, that thought the summer's name
Some rumor of delirium
No summer could for them;

Or Arctic creature, dimly stirred
By tropic hint, — some travelled bird
Imported to the wood;

Or wind's bright signal to the ear,
Making that homely and severe,
Contented, known, before

The heaven unexpected came,
To lives that thought their worshipping
A too presumptuous psalm.

If what we could were what we would —
Criterion be small;
It is the Ultimate of talk
The impotence to tell.

For Death, — or rather
For the things 'twill buy,
These put away
Life's opportunity.

The things that Death will buy
Are Room, — Escape
From Circumstances,
And a Name.
How gifts of Life
With Death's gifts will compare,
We know not —
For the rates stop Here.

If recollecting were forgetting,
    Then I remember not;
And if forgetting, recollecting,
    How near I had forgot!
And if to miss were merry,
    And if to mourn were gay,
How very blithe the fingers
    That gathered these to-day!

I send two Sunsets —
Day and I in competition ran,
I finished two, and several stars,
While He was making one.

His own is ampler —
But, as I was saying to a friend,
Mine is the more convenient
To carry in the hand.

I had been hungry all the years;
My noon had come, to dine;
I, trembling, drew the table near,
And touched the curious wine.

'Twas this on the tables I had seen,
When turning, hungry, lone,
I looked in windows, for the wealth
I could not hope to own.

I did not know the ample bread,
'Twas so unlike the crumb
The birds and I had often shared
In Nature's dining-room.

The plenty hurt me, 'twas so new, —
Myself felt ill and odd,
As berry of a mountain bush
Transplanted to the road.

Nor was I hungry; so I found
That hunger was a way
Of persons outside windows,
The entering takes away.

Each that we lose takes part of us;
A crescent still abides,
Which like the moon, some turbid night,
Is summoned by the tides.

Good night! which put the candle out?
A jealous zephyr, not a doubt.
    Ah! friend, you little knew
How long at that celestial wick
The angels labored diligent;
    Extinguished, now, for you!

It might have been the lighthouse spark
Some sailor, rowing in the dark,
    Had importuned to see!
It might have been the waning lamp
That lit the drummer from the camp
    To purer reveille!

The mountain sat upon the plain
In his eternal chair,
His observation omnifold,
His inquest everywhere.

The seasons played around his knees,
Like children round a sire;
Grandfather of the days is he,
Of dawn the ancestor.

It was not death, for I stood up,
And all the dead lie down;
It was not night, for all the bells
Put out their tongues, for noon.

It was not frost, for on my flesh
I felt siroccos crawl, —
Nor fire, for just my marble feet
Could keep a chancel cool.

And yet it tasted like them all;
The figures I have seen
Set orderly, for burial,
Reminded me of mine,

As if my life were shaven
And fitted to a frame,
And could not breathe without a key;
And 'twas like midnight, some,

When everything that ticked has stopped,
And space stares, all around,
Or grisly frosts, first autumn morns,
Repeal the beating ground.

But most like chaos, — stopless, cool, —
Without a chance or spar,
Or even a report of land
To justify despair.

I reason, earth is short,
And anguish absolute.
And many hurt;
But what of that?

I reason, we could die:
The best vitality
Cannot excel decay;
But what of that?

I reason that in heaven
Somehow, it will be even,
Some new equation given;
But what of that?

Love reckons by itself alone,
"As large as I" relate the Sun
To one who never felt it blaze,
Itself is all the like it has.

13

The body grows outside, —
The more convenient way, —
That if the spirit like to hide,
Its temple stands alway

Ajar, secure, inviting;
It never did betray
The soul that asked its shelter
In timid honesty.

A door just opened on a street —
   I, lost, was passing by —
An instant's width of warmth disclosed,
   And wealth, and company.

The door as sudden shut, and I,
   I, lost, was passing by, —
Lost doubly, but by contrast most,
   Enlightening misery.

The bee is not afraid of me,
I know the butterfly;
The pretty people in the woods
Receive me cordially.

The brooks laugh louder when I come,
The breezes madder play,
Wherefore, mine eyes, thy silver mists?
Wherefore, O summer's day?

How happy is the little stone
That rambles in the road alone,
And doesn't care about careers,
And exigencies never fears;
Whose coat of elemental brown
A passing universe put on;
And independent as the sun,
Associates or glows alone,
Fulfilling absolute decree
In casual simplicity.

Surgeons must be very careful
When they take the knife!
Underneath their fine incisions
Stirs the culprit, — Life!

The cricket sang,
And set the sun,
And workmen finished, one by one,
   Their seam the day upon.

The low grass loaded with the dew,
The twilight stood as strangers do
With hat in hand, polite and new,
   To stay as if, or go.

A vastness, as a neighbor, came, —
A wisdom without face or name,
A peace, as hemispheres at home, —
   And so the night became.

A word is dead
When it is said,
    Some say,
I say it just
Begins to live
    That day.

❧

There is a word
Which bears a sword
    Can pierce an armed man.
It hurls its barbed syllables, —
    At once is mute again.
But where it fell
The saved will tell
    On patriotic day,
Some epauletted brother
    Gave his breath away.
Wherever runs the breathless sun,
    Wherever roams the day,
There is its noiseless onset,
    There is its victory!
Behold the keenest marksman!
    The most accomplished shot!
Time's sublimest target
    Is a soul "forgot"!

❧

The bustle in a house
The morning after death
Is solemnest of industries
Enacted upon earth, —

The sweeping up the heart,
And putting love away
We shall not want to use again
Until eternity.

A thought went up my mind today
That I have had before,
But did not finish, — some way back,
I could not fix the year,

Nor where it went, nor why it came
The second time to me,
Nor definitely what it was,
Have I the art to say.

But somewhere in my soul, I know
I've met the thing before;
It just reminded me — 'twas all —
And came my way no more.

There came a wind like a bugle;
It quivered through the grass,
And a green chill upon the heat
So ominous did pass
We barred the windows and the doors
As from an emerald ghost;
The doom's electric moccason
That very instant passed.
On a strange mob of panting trees,
And fences fled away,
And rivers where the houses ran
The living looked that day.
The bell within the steeple wild
The flying tidings whirled.
How much can come
And much can go,
And yet abide the world!

I died for beauty, but was scarce
Adjusted in the tomb,
When one who died for truth was lain
In an adjoining room.

He questioned softly why I failed?
"For beauty," I replied.
"And I for truth, — the two are one;
We brethren are," he said.

And so, as kinsmen met a night,
We talked between the rooms,
Until the moss had reached our lips,
And covered up our names.

I lived on dread; to those who know
The stimulus there is
In danger, other impetus
Is numb and vital-less.

As 'twere a spur upon the soul,
A fear will urge it where
To go without the spectre's aid
Were challenging despair.

I think that the root of the Wind is Water,
It would not sound so deep
Were it a firmamental product,
Airs no Oceans keep —
Mediterranean intonations,
To a Current's ear
There is a maritime conviction
In the atmosphere.

It tossed and tossed, —
A little brig I knew, —
O'ertook by blast,
It spun and spun,
And groped delirious, for morn.

It slipped and slipped,
As one that drunken stepped;
Its white foot tripped,
Then dropped from sight.

Ah, brig, good-night
To crew and you;
The ocean's heart too smooth, too blue,
To break for you.

My life closed twice before its close;
　　It yet remains to see
If Immortality unveil
　　A third event to me,

So huge, so hopeless to conceive,
　　As these that twice befell.
Parting is all we know of heaven,
　　And all we need of hell.

Nature rarer uses yellow
Than another hue;
Saves she all of that for sunsets, —
　　Prodigal of blue,

Spending scarlet like a woman,
　　Yellow she affords
Only scantly and selectly,
　　Like a lover's words.

Is bliss, then, such abyss
I must not put my foot amiss
For fear I spoil my shoe?

I'd rather suit my foot
Than save my boot,
For yet to buy another pair
Is possible
At any fair.

But bliss is sold just once;
The patent lost
None buy it any more.

She sweeps with many-colored brooms,
And leaves the shreds behind;
Oh, housewife in the evening west,
Come back, and dust the pond!

You dropped a purple ravelling in,
You dropped an amber thread;
And now you've littered all the East
With duds of emerald!

And still she plies her spotted brooms,
And still the aprons fly,
Till brooms fade softly into stars —
And then I come away.

We learn in the retreating
    How vast an one
Was recently among us.
    A perished sun

Endears in the departure
    How doubly more
Than all the golden presence
    It was before!

No rack can torture me,
My soul's at liberty.
Behind this mortal bone
There knits a bolder one

You cannot prick with saw,
Nor rend with scymitar.
Two bodies therefore be;
Bind one, and one will flee.

The eagle of his nest
No easier divest
And gain the sky,
Than mayest thou,

Except thyself may be
Thine enemy;
Captivity is consciousness,
So's liberty.

So set its sun in thee
What day is dark to me —
What distance far,
So I the ships may see
That touch how seldomly
Thy shore?

A clock stopped — not the mantel's;
    Geneva's farthest skill
Can't put the puppet bowing
    That's just now dangled still.

An awe came on the trinket!
    The figures hunched with pain,
Then quivered out of decimals
    Into degreeless noon.

It will not stir for doctors,
    This pendulum of snow;
The shopman importunes it,
    While cool, concernless No

Nods from the gilded pointers,
    Nods from the seconds slim,
Decades of arrogance between
    The dial life and him.

Some things that fly there be, —
Birds, hours, the bumblebee:
Of these no elegy.

Some things that stay there be, —
Grief, hills, eternity:
Nor this behooveth me.

There are, that resting, rise.
Can I expound the skies?
How still the riddle lies!

Perception of an
Object costs
Precise the Object's loss.
Perception in itself a gain
Replying to its price;
The Object Absolute is nought,
Perception sets it fair,
And then upbraids a Perfectness
That situates so far.

A bird came down the walk:
He did not know I saw;
He bit an angle-worm in halves
And ate the fellow, raw.

And then he drank a dew
From a convenient grass,
And then hopped sidewise to the wall
To let a beetle pass.

He glanced with rapid eyes
That hurried all abroad, —
They looked like frightened beads, I thought
He stirred his velvet head

Like one in danger; cautious,
I offered him a crumb,
And he unrolled his feathers
And rowed him softer home

Than oars divide the ocean,
Too silver for a seam,
Or butterflies, off banks of noon,
Leap, plashless, as they swim.

I've got an arrow here;
    Loving the hand that sent it,
I the dart revere.

Fell, they will say, in "skirmish"!
    Vanquished, my soul will know,
By but a simple arrow
    Sped by an archer's bow.

Adventure most unto itself
The Soul condemned to be;
Attended by a Single Hound —
Its own Identity.

I never hear the word "escape"
Without a quicker blood,
A sudden expectation,
A flying attitude.

I never hear of prisons broad
By soldier battered down,
But I tug childish at my bars, —
Only to fail again!

My country need not change her gown,
Her triple suit as sweet
As when 'twas cut at Lexington,
And first pronounced "a fit."

Great Britain disapproves "the stars";
Disparagement discreet, —
There's something in their attitude
That taunts her bayonet.

There is another Loneliness
That many die without,
Not want or friend occasions it,
Or circumstances or lot.

But nature sometimes, sometimes thought,
And whoso it befall
Is richer than could be divulged
By mortal numeral.

You've seen balloons set, haven't you?
　　So stately they ascend
It is as swans discarded you
　　For duties diamond.

Their liquid feet go softly out
　　Upon a sea of blond;
They spurn the air as 'twere too mean
　　For creatures so renowned.

Their ribbons just beyond the eye,
　　They struggle some for breath,
And yet the crowd applauds below;
　　They would not encore death.

The gilded creature strains and spins,
　　Trips frantic in a tree,
Tears open her imperial veins
　　And tumbles in the sea.

The crowd retire with an oath
　　The dust in streets goes down,
And clerks in counting-rooms observe
　　"'Twas only a balloon."

It's like the light, —
    A fashionless delight,
It's like the bee, —
    A dateless melody.

It's like the woods,
    Private like breeze,
Phraseless, yet it stirs
    The proudest trees.

It's like the morning, —
    Best when it's done, —
The everlasting clocks
    Chime noon.

As imperceptibly as grief
The summer lapsed away, —
Too imperceptible, at last,
To seem like perfidy.

A quietness distilled,
As twilight long begun,
Or Nature, spending with herself
Sequestered afternoon.

The dusk drew earlier in,
The morning foreign shone, —
A courteous, yet harrowing grace,
As guest who would be gone.

And thus, without a wing,
Or service of a keel,
Our summer made her light escape
Into the beautiful.

Softened by Time's consummate plush,
    How sleek the woe appears
That threatened childhood's citadel
    And undermined the years!

Bisected now by bleaker griefs,
    We envy the despair
That devastated childhood's realm,
    So easy to repair.

The long sigh of the Frog
Upon a Summer's day,
Enacts intoxication
Upon the revery.
But his receding swell
Substantiates a peace,
That makes the ear inordinate
For corporal release.

Before I got my eye put out,
I liked as well to see
As other creatures that have eyes,
And know no other way.

But were it told to me, to-day,
That I might have the sky
For mine, I tell you that my heart
Would split, for size of me.

The meadows mine, the mountains mine, —
All forests, stintless stars,
As much of noon as I could take
Between my finite eyes.

The motions of the dipping birds,
The lightning's jointed road,
For mine to look at when I liked, —
The news would strike me dead!

So, safer, guess, with just my soul
Upon the window-pane
Where other creatures put their eyes,
Incautious of the sun.

I heard a fly buzz when I died;
　　The stillness round my form
Was like the stillness in the air
　　Between the heaves of storm.

The eyes beside had wrung them dry,
　　And breaths were gathering sure
For that last onset, when the king
　　Be witnessed in his power.

I willed my keepsakes, signed away
　　What portion of me I
Could make assignable, — and then
　　There interposed a fly,

With blue, uncertain, stumbling buzz,
　　Between the light and me;
And then the windows failed, and then
　　I could not see to see.

What if I say I shall not wait?
What if I burst the fleshly gate
And pass, escaped, to thee?
What if I file this mortal off,
See where it hurt me, — that's enough, —
And wade in liberty?

They cannot take us any more, —
Dungeons may call, and guns implore;
Unmeaning now, to me,
As laughter was an hour ago,
Or laces, or a travelling show,
Or who died yesterday!

To tell the beauty would decrease,
To state the Spell demean,
There is a syllableless sea
Of which it is the sign.

My will endeavours for its word
And fails, but entertains
A rapture as of legacies —
Of introspective mines.

I started early, took my dog,
And visited the sea;
The mermaids in the basement
Came out to look at me,

And frigates in the upper floor
Extended hempen hands,
Presuming me to be a mouse
Aground, upon the sands.

But no man moved me till the tide
Went past my simple shoe,
And past my apron and my belt,
And past my bodice too,

And made as he would eat me up
As wholly as a dew
Upon a dandelion's sleeve —
And then I started too.

And he — he followed close behind;
I felt his silver heel
Upon my ankle, — then my shoes
Would overflow with pearl.

Until we met the solid town,
No man he seemed to know;
And bowing with a mighty look
At me, the sea withdrew.

Give little anguish
Lives will fret.
Give avalanches —
And they 'll slant,
Straighten, look cautious for their breath,
But make no syllable —
Like Death,
   Who only shows his
   Marble disc —
Sublimer sort than speech.

I years had been from home,
And now, before the door,
I dared not open, lest a face
I never saw before

Stare vacant into mine
And ask my business there.
My business, — just a life I left,
Was such still dwelling there?

I fumbled at my nerve,
I scanned the windows near;
The silence like an ocean rolled,
And broke against my ear.

I laughed a wooden laugh
That I could fear a door,
Who danger and the dead had faced,
But never quaked before.

I fitted to the latch
My hand, with trembling care,
Lest back the awful door should spring,
And leave me standing there.

I moved my fingers off
As cautiously as glass,
And held my ears, and like a thief
Fled gasping from the house.

Mine enemy is growing old, —
I have at last revenge.
The palate of the hate departs;
If any would avenge, —

Let him be quick, the viand flits,
It is a faded meat.
Anger as soon as fed is dead;
'Tis starving makes it fat.

Remembrance has a rear and front, —
    'Tis something like a house;
It has a garret also
    For refuse and the mouse,

Besides, the deepest cellar
    That ever mason hewed;
Look to it, by its fathoms
    Ourselves be not pursued.

I measure every grief I meet
   With analytic eyes;
I wonder if it weighs like mine,
   Or has an easier size.

I wonder if they bore it long,
   Or did it just begin?
I could not tell the date of mine,
   It feels so old a pain.

I wonder if it hurts to live,
   And if they have to try,
And whether, could they choose between,
   They would not rather die.

I wonder if when years have piled —
   Some thousands — on the cause
Of early hurt, if such a lapse
   Could give them any pause;

Or would they go on aching still
   Through centuries above,
Enlightened to a larger pain
   By contrast with the love.

The grieved are many, I am told;
   The reason deeper lies, —
Death is but one and comes but once,
   And only nails the eyes.

There's grief of want, and grief of cold, —
    A sort they call "despair";
There's banishment from native eyes,
    In sight of native air.

And though I may not guess the kind
    Correctly, yet to me
A piercing comfort it affords
    In passing Calvary,

To note the fashions of the cross,
    Of those that stand alone,
Still fascinated to presume
    That some are like my own.

44

Pain has an element of blank;
It cannot recollect
When it began, or if there were
A day when it was not.

It has no future but itself,
Its infinite realms contain
Its past, enlightened to perceive
New periods of pain.

Apparently with no surprise
To any happy flower,
The frost beheads it at its play
In accidental power.

The blond assassin passes on,
The sun proceeds unmoved
To measure off another day
For an approving God.

At half-past three a single bird
Unto a silent sky
Propounded but a single term
Of cautious melody.

At half-past four, experiment
Had subjugated test,
And lo! her silver principle
Supplanted all the rest.

At half-past seven, element
Nor implement was seen,
And place was where the presence was,
Circumference between.

My river runs to thee:
Blue sea, wilt welcome me?

My river waits reply
Oh sea, look graciously!

I 'll fetch thee brooks
From spotted nooks, —

Say, sea,
Take me!

The last night that she lived,
It was a common night,
Except the dying; this to us
Made nature different.

We noticed smallest things, —
Things overlooked before,
By this great light upon our minds
Italicized, as 'twere.

That others could exist
While she must finish quite,
A jealousy for her arose
So nearly infinite.

We waited while she passed;
It was a narrow time,
Too jostled were our souls to speak,
At length the notice came.

She mentioned, and forgot;
Then lightly as a reed
Bent to the water, shivered scarce,
Consented, and was dead.

And we, we placed the hair,
And drew the head erect;
And then an awful leisure was,
Our faith to regulate.

The sun kept setting, setting still;
No hue of afternoon
Upon the village I perceived, —
From house to house 'twas noon.

The dusk kept dropping, dropping still;
No dew upon the grass,
But only on my forehead stopped,
And wandered in my face.

My feet kept drowsing, drowsing still,
My fingers were awake;
Yet why so little sound myself
Unto my seeming make?

How well I knew the light before!
I could not see it now.
'Tis dying, I am doing; but
I'm not afraid to know.

The murmuring of bees has ceased;
    But murmuring of some
Posterior, prophetic,
    Has simultaneous come, —

The lower metres of the year,
    When nature's laugh is done, —
The Revelations of the book
    Whose Genesis is June.

If I can stop one heart from breaking,
I shall not live in vain;
If I can ease one life the aching,
Or cool one pain,
Or help one fainting robin
Unto his nest again,
I shall not live in vain.

A narrow fellow in the grass
Occasionally rides;
You may have met him, — did you not?
His notice sudden is.

The grass divides as with a comb,
A spotted shaft is seen;
And then it closes at your feet
And opens further on.

He likes a boggy acre,
A floor too cool for corn,
Yet when a child, and barefoot,
I more than once, at morn,

Have passed, I thought, a whip-lash
Unbraiding in the sun, —
When, stooping to secure it,
It wrinkled, and was gone.

Several of nature's people
I know, and they know me;
I feel for them a transport
Of cordiality;

But never met his fellow,
Attended or alone,
Without a tighter breathing,
And zero at the bone.

There's a certain slant of light,
On winter afternoons,
That oppresses, like the weight
Of cathedral tunes.

Heavenly hurt it gives us;
We can find no scar,
But internal difference
Where the meanings are.

None may teach it anything,
'Tis the seal, despair, —
An imperial affliction
Sent us of the air.

When it comes, the landscape listens,
Shadows hold their breath;
When it goes, 'tis like the distance
On the look of death.

A toad can die of light!
Death is the common right
　　Of toads and men, —
Of earl and midge

The privilege.
　　Why swagger then?
The gnat's supremacy
Is large as thine.

Low at my problem bending,
Another problem comes,
Larger than mine, serener,
Involving statelier sums;
I check my busy pencil,
My ciphers slip away,
Wherefore, my baffled fingers,
Time Eternity?

I gained it so,
By climbing slow,
By catching at the twigs that grow
Between the bliss and me.
It hung so high,
As well the sky
Attempt by strategy.

I said I gained it, —
This was all.
Look, how I clutch it,
Lest it fall,
And I a pauper go;
Unfitted by an instant's grace
For the contented beggar's face
I wore an hour ago.

My Wheel is in the dark, —
I cannot see a spoke,
Yet know its dripping feet
Go round and round.

My foot is on the tide —
An unfrequented road,
Yet have all roads
A "clearing" at the end.

Some have resigned the Loom,
Some in the busy tomb
Find quaint employ,
Some with new, stately feet
Pass royal through the gate,
Flinging the problem back at you and I.

Much madness is divinest sense
To a discerning eye;
Much sense the starkest madness.
'Tis the majority
In this, as all, prevails.
Assent, and you are sane;
Demur, — you're straightway dangerous,
And handled with a chain.

∼⁓∽

The soul unto itself
Is an imperial friend, —
Or the most agonizing spy
An enemy could send.

Secure against its own,
No treason it can fear;
Itself its sovereign, of itself
The soul should stand in awe.

∼⁓∽

Her Grace is all she has,
And that, so vast displays,
One Art, to recognize, must be,
Another Art to praise.

∼⁓∽

I felt a funeral in my brain,
    And mourners, to and fro,
Kept treading, treading, till it seemed
    That sense was breaking through.

And when they all were seated,
    A service like a drum
Kept beating, beating, till I thought
    My mind was going numb.

And then I heard them lift a box,
    And creak across my soul
With those same boots of lead, again.
    Then space began to toll

As all the heavens were a bell,
    And Being but an ear,
And I and silence some strange race,
    Wrecked, solitary, here.

Wild nights! Wild nights!
Were I with thee,
Wild nights should be
Our luxury!

Futile the winds
To a heart in port, —
Done with the compass,
Done with the chart.

Rowing in Eden!
Ah! the sea!
Might I but moor
Tonight in thee!

Not any sunny tone
From any fervent zone
Finds entrance there.
Better a grave of Balm
Toward human nature's home,
And Robins near,
Than a stupendous Tomb
Proclaiming to the gloom
How dead we are.

The Soul's superior instants
Occur to Her alone,
When friend and earth's occasion
Have infinite withdrawn.

Or she, Herself, ascended
To too remote a height,
For lower recognition
Than Her Omnipotent.

This mortal abolition
Is seldom, but as fair
As Apparition — subject
To autocratic air.

Eternity's disclosure
To favorites, a few,
Of the Colossal substance
Of immortality.

A death-blow is a life-blow to some
Who, till they died, did not alive become;
Who, had they lived, had died, but when
They died, vitality begun.

You cannot put a fire out;
    A thing that can ignite
Can go, itself, without a fan
    Upon the slowest night.

You cannot fold a flood
    And put it in a drawer, —
Because the winds would find it out,
    And tell your cedar floor.

It dropped so low in my regard
    I heard it hit the ground,
And go to pieces on the stones
    At bottom of my mind;

Yet blamed the fate that fractured, less
    Than I reviled myself
For entertaining plated wares
    Upon my silver shelf.

Love is anterior to life,
Posterior to death,
Initial of creation, and
    The exponent of breath.

Of all the sounds despatched abroad,
There's not a charge to me
Like that old measure in the boughs,
That phraseless melody

The wind does, working like a hand
Whose fingers comb the sky,
Then quiver down, with tufts of tune
Permitted gods and me.

When winds go round and round in bands,
And thrum upon the door,
And birds take places overhead,
To bear them orchestra,

I crave him grace, of summer boughs,
If such an outcast be,
He never heard that fleshless chant
Rise solemn in the tree,

As if some caravan of sound
On deserts, in the sky,
Had broken rank,
Then knit, and passed
In seamless company.

A precious, mouldering pleasure 'tis
To meet an antique book,
In just the dress his century wore;
A privilege, I think,

His venerable hand to take,
And warming in our own,
A passage back, or two, to make
To times when he was young.

His quaint opinions to inspect,
His knowledge to unfold
On what concerns our mutual mind,
The literature of old;

What interested scholars most,
What competitions ran
When Plato was a certainty,
And Sophocles a man;

When Sappho was a living girl,
And Beatrice wore
The gown that Dante deified.
Facts, centuries before,

He traverses familiar,
As one should come to town
And tell you all your dreams were true:
He lived where dreams were born.

His presence is enchantment,
You beg him not to go;
Old volumes shake their vellum heads
And tantalize, just so.

This world is not conclusion;
   A sequel stands beyond,
Invisible, as music,
   But positive, as sound.
It beckons and it baffles;
   Philosophies don't know,
And through a riddle, at the last,
   Sagacity must go.
To guess it puzzles scholars;
   To gain it, men have shown
Contempt of generations,
   And crucifixion known.

That Love is all there is,
Is all we know of Love;
It is enough, the freight should be
Proportioned to the groove.

I felt a cleavage in my mind
    As if my brain had split;
I tried to match it, seam by seam,
    But could not make them fit.

The thought behind I strove to join
    Unto the thought before,
But sequence ravelled out of reach
    Like balls upon a floor.

Except the heaven had come so near,
So seemed to choose my door,
The distance would not haunt me so;
I had not hoped before.

But just to hear the grace depart
I never thought to see
Afflicts me with a double loss;
'Tis lost, and lost to me.

Exultation is the going
Of an inland soul to sea, —
Past the houses, past the headlands,
Into deep eternity!

Bred as we, among the mountains,
Can the sailor understand
The divine intoxication
Of the first league out from land?

The brain is wider than the sky,
    For, put them side by side,
The one the other will include
    With ease, and you beside.

The brain is deeper than the sea,
    For, hold them, blue to blue,
The one the other will absorb,
    As sponges, buckets do.

The brain is just the weight of God,
    For, lift them, pound for pound,
And they will differ, if they do,
    As syllable from sound.

An everywhere of silver,
With ropes of sand
To keep it from effacing
The track called land.

Could I but ride indefinite,
    As doth the meadow-bee,
And visit only where I liked,
    And no man visit me,

And flirt all day with buttercups,
    And marry whom I may,
And dwell a little everywhere,
    Or better, run away

With no police to follow,
    Or chase me if I do,
Till I should jump peninsulas
    To get away from you, —

I said, but just to be a bee
    Upon a raft of air,
And row in nowhere all day long,
    And anchor off the bar, —
What liberty! So captives deem
    Who tight in dungeons are.

The moon was but a chin of gold
   A night or two ago,
And now she turns her perfect face
   Upon the world below.

Her forehead is of amplest blond;
   Her cheek like beryl stone;
Her eye unto the summer dew
   The likest I have known.

Her lips of amber never part;
   But what must be the smile
Upon her friend she could bestow
   Were such her silver will!

And what a privilege to be
   But the remotest star!
For certainly her way might pass
   Beside your twinkling door.

Her bonnet is the firmament,
   The universe her shoe,
The stars the trinkets at her belt,
   Her dimities of blue.

Not knowing when the dawn will come
   I open every door;
Or has it feathers like a bird,
   Or billows like a shore?

I dreaded that first robin so,
But he is mastered now,
And I'm accustomed to him grown, —
He hurts a little, though.

I thought if I could only live
Till that first shout got by,
Not all pianos in the woods
Had power to mangle me.

I dared not meet the daffodils,
For fear their yellow gown
Would pierce me with a fashion
So foreign to my own.

I wished the grass would hurry,
So when 'twas time to see,
He'd be too tall, the tallest one
Could stretch to look at me.

I could not bear the bees should come,
I wished they'd stay away
In those dim countries where they go:
What word had they for me?

They're here, though; not a creature failed,
No blossom stayed away
In gentle deference to me,
The Queen of Calvary.

Each one salutes me as he goes,
And I my childish plumes
Lift, in bereaved acknowledgment
Of their unthinking drums.

Of bronze and blaze
The north, to-night!
   So adequate its forms,
So preconcerted with itself,
   So distant to alarms, —
An unconcern so sovereign
   To universe, or me,
It paints my simple spirit
   With tints of majesty,
Till I take vaster attitudes,
   And strut upon my stem,
Disdaining men and oxygen,
   For arrogance of them.

My splendors are menagerie;
   But their completeless show
Will entertain the centuries
   When I am, long ago,
An island in dishonored grass,
   Whom none but daisies know.

At last to be identified!
At last, the lamps upon thy side,
The rest of life to see!
Past midnight, past the morning star!
Past sunrise! Ah! what leagues there are
Between our feet and day!

To lose one's faith surpasses
    The loss of an estate,
Because estates can be
    Replenished, — faith cannot.

Inherited with life,
    Belief but once can be;
Annihilate a single clause,
    And Being's beggary.

We play at paste,
Till qualified for pearl,
Then drop the paste,
And deem ourself a fool.
The shapes, though, were similar,
And our new hands
Learned gem-tactics
Practising sands.

The rat is the concisest tenant.
He pays no rent, —
Repudiates the obligation,
On schemes intent.

Balking our wit
To sound or circumvent,
Hate cannot harm
A foe so reticent.

Neither decree
Prohibits him,
Lawful as
Equilibrium.

Superiority to fate
　　Is difficult to learn.
'Tis not conferred by any,
　　But possible to earn.

A pittance at a time,
　　Until, to her surprise,
The soul with strict economy
　　Subsists till Paradise.

Hope is the thing with feathers
That perches in the soul,
And sings the tune without the words,
And never stops at all,

And sweetest in the gale is heard;
And sore must be the storm
That could abash the little bird
That kept so many warm.

I've heard it in the chillest land,
And on the strangest sea;
Yet, never, in extremity,
It asked a crumb of me.

The missing All prevented me
From missing minor things.
If nothing larger than a World's
Departure from a hinge,
Or Sun's extinction be observed,
'Twas not so large that I
Could lift my forehead from my work
For curiosity.

I breathed enough to learn the trick,
    And now, removed from air,
I simulate the breath so well,
    That one, to be quite sure

The lungs are stirless, must descend
    Among the cunning cells,
And touch the pantomime himself.
    How cool the bellows feels!

This was in the white of the year,
    That was in the green,
Drifts were as difficult then to think
    As daisies now to be seen.

Looking back is best that is left,
    Or if it be before,
Retrospection is prospect's half,
    Sometimes almost more.

The largest fire ever known
Occurs each afternoon,
Discovered is without surprise,
Proceeds without concern:
Consumes, and no report to men,
An Occidental town,
Rebuilt another morning
To be again burned down.

Had this one day not been,
Or could it cease to be —
How smitten, how superfluous
Were every other day!

Lest Love should value less
What Loss would value more,
Had it the stricken privilege —
It cherishes before.

I never saw a moor,
I never saw the sea;
Yet know I how the heather looks,
And what a wave must be.

I never spoke with God,
Nor visited in heaven;
Yet certain am I of the spot
As if the chart were given.

One need not be a chamber to be haunted,
One need not be a house;
The brain has corridors surpassing
Material place.

Far safer, of a midnight meeting
External ghost,
Than an interior confronting
That whiter host.

Far safer through an Abbey gallop,
The stone achase,
Than, moonless, one's own self encounter
In lonesome place.

Ourself, behind ourself concealed,
Should startle most;
Assassin, hid in our apartment,
Be horror's least.

The prudent carries a revolver,
He bolts the door,
O'erlooking a superior spectre
More near.

Split the lark and you'll find the music,
    Bulb after bulb, in silver rolled,
Scantily dealt to the summer morning,
    Saved for your ear when lutes be old.

Loose the flood, you shall find it patent,
    Gush after gush, reserved for you;
Scarlet experiment! sceptic Thomas,
    Now, do you doubt that your bird was true?

My cocoon tightens, colors tease,
I'm feeling for the air;
A dim capacity for wings
Degrades the dress I wear.

A power of butterfly must be
The aptitude to fly,
Meadows of majesty concedes
And easy sweeps of sky.

So I must baffle at the hint
And cipher at the sign,
And make much blunder, if at last
I take the clue divine.

The murmur of a bee
A witchcraft yieldeth me.
If any ask me why,
'Twere easier to die
Than tell.

The red upon the hill
Taketh away my will;
If anybody sneer,
Take care, for God is here,
That's all.

The breaking of the day
Addeth to my degree;
If any ask me how,
Artist, who drew me so,
Must tell!

I had no time to hate, because
The grave would hinder me,
And life was not so ample I
Could finish enmity.

Nor had I time to love; but since
Some industry must be,
The little toil of love, I thought,
Was large enough for me.

What mystery pervades a well!
    The water lives so far,
Like neighbor from another world
    Residing in a jar.

The grass does not appear afraid;
    I often wonder he
Can stand so close and look so bold
    At what is dread to me.

Related somehow they may be, —
    The sedge stands next the sea,
Where he is floorless, yet of fear
    No evidence gives he.

But nature is a stranger yet;
    The ones that cite her most
Have never passed her haunted house,
    Nor simplified her ghost.

To pity those that know her not
    Is helped by the regret
That those who know her, know her less
    The nearer her they get.

There is a solitude of space,
A solitude of sea,
A solitude of death, but these
Society shall be,
Compared with that profounder site,
That polar privacy,
A Soul admitted to Itself:
Finite Infinity.

Great streets of silence led away
To neighborhoods of pause;
Here was no notice, no dissent,
No universe, no laws.

By clocks 'twas morning, and for night
The bells at distance called;
But epoch had no basis here,
For period exhaled.

Experiment to me
Is every one I meet.
If it contain a kernel?
The figure of a nut

Presents upon a tree,
Equally plausibly;
But meat within is requisite,
To squirrels and to me.

Dear March, come in!
How glad I am!
I looked for you before.
Put down your hat —
You must have walked —
How out of breath you are!
Dear March, how are you?
And the rest?
Did you leave Nature well?
Oh, March, come right upstairs with me,
I have so much to tell!

I got your letter, and the bird's;
The maples never knew
That you were coming, — I declare,
How red their faces grew!
But, March, forgive me —
And all those hills
You left for me to hue;
There was no purple suitable,
You took it all with you.

Who knocks? That April!
Lock the door!
I will not be pursued!
He stayed away a year, to call
When I am occupied.
But trifles look so trivial
As soon as you have come.
That blame is just as dear as praise
And praise as mere as blame.

Heart not so heavy as mine,
Wending late home,
As it passed my window
Whistled itself a tune, —

A careless snatch, a ballad,
A ditty of the street;
Yet to my irritated ear
An anodyne so sweet,

It was as if a bobolink,
Sauntering this way,
Carolled and mused and carolled,
Then bubbled slow away.

It was as if a chirping brook
Upon a toilsome way
Set bleeding feet to minuets
Without the knowing why.

To-morrow, night will come again,
Weary, perhaps, and sore.
Ah, bugle, by my window,
I pray you stroll once more!

91

While I was fearing it, it came,
    But came with less of fear,
Because that fearing it so long
    Had almost made it dear.
There is a fitting a dismay,
    A fitting a despair,
'Tis harder knowing it is due,
    Than knowing it is here.
The trying on the utmost,
    The morning it is new,
Is terribler than wearing it
    A whole existence through.

Delight becomes pictorial
When viewed through pain, —
More fair, because impossible
That any gain.

The mountain at a given distance
In amber lies;
Approached, the amber flits a little, —
And that's the skies!

It struck me every day
    The lightning was as new
As if the cloud that instant slit
    And let the fire through.

It burned me in the night,
    It blistered in my dream;
It sickened fresh upon my sight
    With every morning's beam.

I thought that storm was brief, —
    The maddest, quickest by;
But Nature lost the date of this,
    And left it in the sky.

I see thee better in the dark,
I do not need a light.
The love of thee a prism be
Excelling violet.

I see thee better for the years
That hunch themselves between,
The miner's lamp sufficient be
To nullify the mine.

And in the grave I see thee best —
Its little panels be
Aglow, all ruddy with the light
I held so high for thee!

What need of day to those whose dark
Hath so surpassing sun,
It seem it be continually
At the meridian?

A wounded deer leaps highest,
I've heard the hunter tell;
'Tis but the ecstasy of death,
And then the brake is still.

The smitten rock that gushes,
The trampled steel that springs:
A cheek is always redder
Just where the hectic stings!

Mirth is the mail of anguish,
In which it caution arm,
Lest anybody spy the blood
And "You're hurt" exclaim!

The one that could repeat the summer day
Were greater than itself, though he
Minutest of mankind might be.
And who could reproduce the sun,
At period of going down —
The lingering and the stain, I mean —
When Orient has been outgrown,
And Occident becomes unknown,
His name remain.

A face devoid of love or grace,
A hateful, hard, successful face,
  A face with which a stone
Would feel as thoroughly at ease
As were they old acquaintances, —
  First time together thrown.

Portraits are to daily faces
As an evening west
To a fine, pedantic sunshine
In a satin vest.

Exhilaration is the Breeze
That lifts us from the ground,
And leaves us in another place
Whose statement is not found;
Returns us not, but after time
We soberly descend,
A little newer for the term
Upon enchanted ground.

Because I could not stop for Death,
He kindly stopped for me;
The carriage held but just ourselves
And Immortality.

We slowly drove, he knew no haste,
And I had put away
My labor, and my leisure too,
For his civility.

We passed the school where children played
At wrestling in a ring;
We passed the fields of gazing grain,
We passed the setting sun.

We paused before a house that seemed
A swelling of the ground;
The roof was scarcely visible,
The cornice but a mound.

Since then 'tis centuries; but each
Feels shorter than the day
I first surmised the horses' heads
Were toward eternity.

After a hundred years
Nobody knows the place, —
Agony, that enacted there,
Motionless as peace.

Weeds triumphant ranged,
Strangers strolled and spelled
At the lone orthography
Of the elder dead.

Winds of summer fields
Recollect the way, —
Instinct picking up the key
Dropped by memory.

❧

The grave my little cottage is,
   Where, keeping house for thee,
I make my parlor orderly,
   And lay the marble tea,

For two divided, briefly,
   A cycle, it may be,
Till everlasting life unite
   In strong society.

❧

I stepped from plank to plank
　　So slow and cautiously;
The stars about my head I felt,
　　About my feet the sea.

I knew not but the next
　　Would be my final inch, —
This gave me that precarious gait
　　Some call experience.

From cocoon forth a butterfly
As lady from her door
Emerged — a summer afternoon —
Repairing everywhere,

Without design, that I could trace
Except to stray abroad
On miscellaneous enterprise
The clovers understood.

Her pretty parasol as seen
Contracting in a field
Where men made hay, then struggling hard
With an opposing cloud,

Where parties, phantom as herself,
To Nowhere seemed to go
In purposeless circumference,
As 'twere a tropic show.

And notwithstanding bee that worked,
And flower that zealous blew,
This audience of idleness
Disdained them, from the sky,

Till sundown crept, a steady tide,
And men that made the hay,
And afternoon, and butterfly,
Extinguished in its sea.

Unto my books so good to turn
Far ends of tired days;
It half endears the abstinence,
And pain is missed in praise.

As flavors cheer retarded guests
With banquetings to be,
So spices stimulate the time
Till my small library.

It may be wilderness without,
Far feet of failing men,
But holiday excludes the night,
And it is bells within.

I thank these kinsmen of the shelf;
Their countenances bland
Enamour in prospective,
And satisfy, obtained.

I many times thought peace had come,
When peace was far away;
As wrecked men deem they sight the land
At centre of the sea,

And struggle slacker, but to prove,
As hopelessly as I,
How many the fictitious shores
Before the harbor lie.

Like trains of cars on tracks of plush
I hear the level bee:
A jar across the flowers goes,
Their velvet masonry

Withstands until the sweet assault
Their chivalry consumes,
While he, victorious, tilts away
To vanquish other blooms.

His feet are shod with gauze,
His helmet is of gold;
His breast, a single onyx
With chrysoprase, inlaid.

His labor is a chant,
His idleness a tune;
Oh, for a bee's experience
Of clovers and of noon!

Just lost when I was saved!
Just felt the world go by!
Just girt me for the onset with eternity,
When breath blew black,
And on the other side
I heard recede the disappointed tide!

Therefore, as one returned, I feel,
Odd secrets of the line to tell!
Some sailor, skirting foreign shores,
Some pale reporter from the awful doors
Before the seal!

Next time, to stay!
Next time, the things to see
By ear unheard,
Unscrutinized by eye.

Next time, to tarry,
While the ages steal, —
Slow tramp the centuries,
And the cycles wheel.

Those final Creatures, — who they are —
That, faithful to the close,
Administer her ecstasy,
But just the Summer knows.

I have no life but this,
To lead it here;
Nor any death, but lest
Dispelled from there;

Nor tie to earths to come,
Nor action new,
Except through this extent,
The realm of you.

About the Author
EMILY DICKINSON

EMILY DICKINSON was born on December 10, 1830, in Amherst, Massachusetts. Her father was the lawyer and treasurer of Amherst College.

Dickinson spent her entire life in Amherst and seldom traveled out of town. She never married and generally avoided personal contact with anyone other than relatives. She did keep up correspondences with a few friends throughout her life, and in her twenties, the style of her letters changed to match the style of her poetry.

Unlike many other writers, Dickinson did not show great interest in publishing her work. Of the more than 2,000 poems she wrote, only a handful were published in her lifetime. Though she often included her poems or lines from poems in letters, no one had any idea how prolific she was until after her death in 1886.

For the remarkable originality in the content and technique of her writing, Emily Dickinson is recognized as one of the greatest American poets.

About the Introduction Author
VIRGINIA EUWER WOLFF

VIRGINIA EUWER WOLFF is the acclaimed author of *True Believer, Make Lemonade, Bat 6, The Mozart Season,* and *Probably Still Nick Swansen.* She lives in Oregon City, Oregon.